MW00698824

MEDITATIONS ON SHIVA

MEDITATIONS ON SHIVA

The *Shivastotravali* of Utpaladeva

Translated by Constantina Rhodes Bailly
Eckerd College

STATE UNIVERSITY OF NEW YORK PRESS

Published by
State University of New York Press, Albany

© 1995 State University of New York

For information, address State University of New York Press,
State University Plaza, Albany, N.Y., 12246

Production by Cathleen Collins
Marketing by Bernadette LaManna

ISBN 0-7914-2530-4

10 9 8 7 6 5 4 3 2

Contents

Introduction

How often in a lifetime is one fortunate enough to encounter even a glimpse of a magnificent, radiant center within?—whether discovered in a dream, a meditation, in the breath of the first balmy and fragrant evening of summer, or in an encounter where the line is finally crossed, where one's heart leaps up and realizes, this is what is right, this is what is true . . . and why have I never recognized this before?

In the first intoxicating flash of such recognition, one may feel like proclaiming ecstatically, as does Utpaladeva in this book, "I roar! Oh, and I dance! / My heart's desires are fulfilled . . . " (3.11). This is the exhilaration of having peeled away layer after layer of debilitating restrictions, and finally being able to experience one's ecstatic center, whose very nature is divine.

And then, having encountered that core of blissful awareness, how does one describe it? Ordinary people blessed with extraordinary experiences usually con-

cede that their language is an insufficient vehicle for
such description. The great sages, returning from that
state and attempting to translate it, have discovered
that the words fall from their lips as poetry. Such are
the devotional songs of Utpaladeva, the great tenth-
century philosopher of the Pratyabhijñā School of
Kashmir. Here, in this collection, are auto-
biographical reflections of his *sādhana*, or spiritual
progress. The format is the Sanskrit *stotra*, a laudatory
and visionary poem or hymn or song directed to the
deity. Composed (or inspired, as has been suggested)
in strict Sanskrit metrical form, these *stotras* are
intended to be sung or chanted. Utpaladeva's disciples
gathered together their *guru*'s devotional poetry and
named the collection the *Śivastotrāvalī*, literally,
"Garland of Songs to Śiva." In the Śaiva philosophies
of Kashmir, Śiva is not only the highest god of all
*deva*s (gods), but is indeed the supreme consciousness
and reality of the entire universe.

     The title of this volume, *Meditations on Shiva*,
acknowledges the contemplative as well as the
devotional aspect of the verses of the *Śivastotrāvalī*,
which range from the pensive to the agonizing to the
ecstatic, and the many points in between to which
sādhana invariably leads. Utpaladeva records his

experiences of what is known in Indian aesthetic theory as *sambhoga*, the sweet and expansive intoxication of encountering the divine beloved. That experience brings simultaneously a sense of both glorious freedom and of steadfast security. But since we are human and perceive the world with varying degrees of "contacted" (*saṃkucita*) consciousness, that ecstatic glimpse is only, in the beginning, a momentary one. When the beloved is said to hide, or when that heightened divine awareness fades, one is said to experience *vipralambha*, the intense agony of separation. To replay in the mind, over and over again, the image and the sensation of one last encounter, one last ecstatic, affirming vision before a consciousness of expansive awareness contracts back to ordinary, limited peceptions—such is the anguish of *vipralambha*.

How are we to interpret Utpaladeva's expressions of delight and of disappointment? What he seeks is a vision of the highest Self. That vision can serve to bring about a transformation in the way the *sādhaka*, or seeker, understands who he is; it can lead to the recognition (*pratyabhijñā*) of one's true identity and the complete merging (*samāveśa*) of limited consciousness into the infinite consciousness of Śiva.

From this, the highest state of realization, the seeker can proclaim, *śivo'ham*, "I am Śiva." Complete identification with the consciousness of the whole universe is the ultimate goal of the *sādhaka*, according to Utpaladeva's philosophy of Pratya-bhijñā. The seeker's awakening and progress in *sādhana* are attributed to "the touch of the *guru*," (5.1), or spiritual preceptor. With the guidance and power of the *guru*, the seeker's ultimate knowledge of the Self begins to unfold, gradually for some and more quickly for others.

Awareness may begin to filter into a dark and heavy consciousness, but the light will not shine steadily at first. To become established in the constant, unwavering experience of the supreme divine consciousness—this is the state of one who is a *siddha*, or perfected being. The *siddha* is one who has attained recognition of his true beloved, his very own Self, who is Śiva, the essence and the consciousness of the whole world. A *siddha* is one who is anchored in that state of awareness, and thus is free—free of the limited perception that prohibits the realization of *sat-cit-ānanda*, or true being, consciousness, and delight. This very world begins to change for the aspirant as the spiritual path is tread. For those who are

completely immersed in the love of Lord Śiva, says
Utpaladeva, " . . . this turbulent ocean of the world/ Is
like a great pleasure-lake/ For their amusement"
(3.15).

Utpaladeva is recognized as a *siddha*; he has
penetrated the veil of limited understanding and
become immersed in the expansive, limitless consciousness of Śiva. It is from this vantage point of
having arrived that he looks back and documents the
vicissitudes of the journey toward perfect understanding.

How does one continue to approach such a
destination? "*Tvad-bhakti*," says Utpaladeva throughout the verses, that is, "your love," or "your
devotion." Loving the divine is a mutual love, for
"your devotion" works both ways: the more love is
poured out, the more it is felt to be received. The
longer it can be relished, the longer and more steadfast
can become the ecstasy of recognition of the Self.

For over one thousand years, Utpaladeva's poetry
has served as a type of guidebook to accompany the
seeker treading the spiritual path. He articulates the
words that others have later used to express their own
otherwise ineffable experiences. These *stotras* docu-
ment the subtle changes in perception of the

sādhaka's world as he or she undergoes personal transformation. Subsequent seekers have found that Utpaladeva's extraordinary journey also lends credence to their own often amazing experiences. The Kashmiri tradition places an even subtler and more germane value on Utpaladeva's poetry, for not only is it said to assist the *sādhaka* in progressing toward the goal, it plays a part in initiating the whole process, claiming that by merely hearing the verses of the *Śivastotrāvalī*, one's entire being becomes purified and is spontaneously set on the path toward liberation.

Highlights of Pratyabhijñā
(The Doctrine of Recognition)

The literature of what is generally known as Kashmir Śaivism traditionally is divided into three branches known as the Āgama Śāstra, Spanda Śāstra, and Pratyabhijñā Śāstra. These are considered to be varying but interdependent approaches to one religious and philosophical system. Often the whole system is known as Trika Śāstra, indicating the unity of the three branches. Just as often, however, the term Pratyabhijñā, or Doctrine of Recognition, because it embodies the main philosophical works of Kashmir Śaivism, has come to represent the whole. The major figures of the Pratyabhijñā Śāstra are Somānanda (*ca.* A.D. 875–925), Utpaladeva (*ca.* 900–950), and Abhinavagupta (*ca.* 950–1000); the three have been labeled respectively as "the founder, the systematizer, and the expounder" of Pratyabhijñā.

The term *pratyabhijñā* is usually translated as *recognition* or *recollection* and has been explained as

the "knowledge" (*jñāna*) to which one "turns back"
(*prati*), and which in turn "faces toward" (*abhi*) the
knower. In this system recognition is the realization
of the identity of the *jīvātman*, or individual self, with
paramātman, the universal self. Pratyabhijñā is
typified by the concept that the one reality is Śiva, and
that Śiva expresses himself through Śakti with infinite
*ābhāsa*s, or manifestations. These manifestations are
categorized as thirty-six *tattva*s, or constituents of the
universe (compare with the twenty-five *tattva*s of
Sāṃkhya); since they are the essence of Śiva, the
*tattva*s are no real less than the five *kañcuka*s
("coverings") and the three *mala*s ("impurities") that
constitute *māyā*, which causes the sense that one does
not belong to the universal essence of Śiva, but
instead has a separate identity.

The world of *saṃsāra* is a product of the
limitations of *māyā*. These limitations cause the
individual to remain bound, with a restricted viewpoint regarding his identity and capacities; this
restriction causes him to forget his true nature.
Pratyabhijñā teaches therefore that in order to
overcome this false viewpoint, one must recognize
that *saṃsāra* is not a separate reality, but is a
manifestation of Śiva. When the individual acquires

the recognition that Śiva not only enjoys *svātantrya*, or freedom, but exists also in everything that is limited and bound, he immediately recognizes that he, in turn, is identified with that which is unlimited and absolutely free.

Recognition implies that on every level, in every aspect of perception and of existence, the individual must recognize his unity with Śiva. If the universe is said to undergo a particular process, this process is necessarily recognized as one that may be experienced by the individual. If Śiva is said to constitute the whole universe, so, then, does the individual. In the explanation of how this operates, the texts emphasize the innate unity of the elements in the universe, and it will be seen that the same terms are applied to the processes of both the ultimate self and the individual one.

It is the nature of Śiva to become immanent and then to disappear continually, and this is done by means of his *śakti*, or power, personified as Śakti, who expands outward and then withdraws again. The *tattva*s, like Śiva himself, are said to be in a constant process of *sṛṣṭi* (creation) and *pralaya* (dissolution). This is also known as *unmeṣa* ("opening out") and *nimeṣa* ("closing down"). When Śiva "opens out" and becomes manifest, he is said to become bound and limited. It is thus in this state that the person of ordinary worldly consciousness remains bound in the world. But by identifying with higher and higher manifestations of Śiva, one can come to recognize the supreme state of Śiva—beyond manifestation—that is the body of consciousness itself. Thus does the bonded person become liberated, enjoying the freedom (*svātantrya*) of following the path of Śiva.

Pratyabhijñā provides a system by which one can work toward *samāveśa*, or immersion, and thus reintegration, by changing his sense of identity from that of the *paśu*, limited or bonded perceiver, to the *pati*, master of all processes. The system recognizes four graded *upāya*s (means, ways, paths); by traveling along these "paths" of Śiva, the aspirant learns to recognize that the "five functions" (*pañcakṛtya*s) of Śiva are functions that operate within himself as well. These eternal functions are *sṛṣṭi* (creation or emanation), *sthiti* (maintenance), *saṃhāra* (reabsorption), *vilaya* or *tirodhāna* (concealment), and *anugraha* (grace). The fifth, *anugraha*, is essential for the process of reintegration. It becomes manifest as the aspirant's devotion (*bhakti*) to the Lord. Thus in the songs of the *Śivastotrāvalī* devotion and grace are

equally important. When the aspirant begins to effect
the merging of his identity, he will recognize that the
very act of his offering of devotion is but another
aspect of the Lord's offering of grace.

Utpaladeva acknowledges that there is an array of
systems claiming to lead to that goal of identifying
with the ultimate. But the only one that he considers
truly efficacious is the path of devotion. In the songs
of the *Śivastotrāvalī* we follow the devotee Utpala on
this path. These songs shed light not only on what a
spiritual quest entails in theory—but they record the
experiences and reflections of one as he travels along
this arduous yet joyful journey.

The Śivastotrāvalī

STOTRA ONE

The Pleasure of Devotion

oṃ

We praise the one who is filled with devotion,
Who meditates not nor recites by the rule,
And yet without any effort at all
Attains the splendor of Śiva.

Though my soul is young
Drinking the nectar of your devotion,
It is yet as one gone grey,
With hair whitened by the dust
Along this journey through the world.

Even the path of worldly living
Becomes blissful for the devotees
Who have obtained your blessing, O Lord,
And who live inside your realm.

When everything in the world is in your form,
How could there be a place
Not suitable for devotees?
Where in the world does their *mantra*
Fail to bear fruit?

Triumphant are they, intoxicated
With the celestial drink of devotion.
They are beyond duality
Yet retain you as "the other."

Only those who are immersed
In the joy of fervent devotion
Know the essence, O Lord,
Of your boundless ocean of bliss.

You alone, O Lord, are the self of all.
And everyone naturally loves his own self.
Thus victorious becomes the one who knows
That devotion is inherent in all.

Lord! When the objective world has dissolved
Through a state of deep meditation,
You stand alone—
And who does not see you then?

But even in the state of differentiation
Between the knower and the known,
You are easily seen by the devotees.

Just as Devī,
Your most beloved, endless pool of bliss,
Is inseparable from you,
So may your devotion alone
Be inseparable from me.

The path of the senses is threefold,
Marked by pleasure, pain, and delusion.
For the devotee this is the path
That leads to your attainment.

The highest state of intellectual knowledge
Has none of the taste of the nectar
Of your devotion.
To me, O Lord, it is like sour wine.

Those who practice the exalted science
Of your devotion
Are the only ones who truly know
The essence of knowledge and ignorance alike.

May this vine of speech,
Rising steadily from the root,
Everywhere adorned with blossoms
And sprinkled with the nectar of devotion,
Yield for me fruit abundant with that sentiment.

"One should worship Śiva by becoming Śiva"
Is the old saying. But the devotees say,
"One should worship Śiva by becoming a devotee."
For they can recognize your essence as nondual,
Even when it is in bodily form.

What for the devoted
Does not serve as an instrument
To attain identification with you?
And what, then, for the spiritually inferior,
Does not serve as an obstacle,
Leading to failure in spiritual attainment?

According to *yoga,* you are obtained
At particular times and in particular places.
This is deception!
Otherwise, how is it that you appear to devotees,
O Lord, under all conditions?

Pratyāhāra and similar practices
Have nothing to do with this unique attainment.
Even in what is merely the yogin's nonmeditative
    state,
The devotees acquire complete union.

Neither *yoga* nor austerities
Nor ceremonial worship
Is recommended on this path to Śiva.
Here, only devotion is extolled.

Within and without, let determinate cognition cease,
Dispelled by the brilliant,
Glowing light of devotion.
Let even the name of anxiety be destroyed
So that I may have direct realization
Of the true nature of all things.

With the single word *Śiva*
Ever resting on the tip of the tongue,
The devotees can enjoy
Even the most complete array of savory delights.

Who else is to be counted
By those resting comfortably in the celestial bliss
Of the cool, pure, tranquil, sweet
Sea of the nectar of devotion?

Lord! Why should someone like me
Not taste of the *mahauṣadhi* herb of devotion,
Whose natural extract
Is called liberation?

O Lord, the wise pray for those fortunes alone
That nourish the capacity to delight
In the bliss of your devotion.

They have experienced inexplicable bliss
In a downpour of devotional nectar.
Even should they fall,
They will not become soiled
With the mire of false attachments
And other such things.

When it ripens, the vine of devotion
Inherently bears fruits, called *siddhi*s;
These begin with *aṇimā* and other powers
And culminate in liberation.

How wonderful it is that the mind, O Lord,
In essence the seed of all suffering,
When doused with the nectar of devotion
Bears the magnificent fruit of beatitude.

STOTRA TWO

Contemplation of the All-Soul

May you be glorified, O Essence of Consciousness,
Appearing in many forms as Agni,
The moon, the sun, Brahmā, Viṣṇu,
The mobile and the immobile.

May you be glorified, O Mighty Fire,
Brilliantly lustrous from smearing the ashes
That remain of the universe,
Your sole oblation.

May you be glorified, O Mild One,
Smooth and brimming with the finest nectar,
O Terrible One who burns away
The entire universe.

May you be glorified, O Mahādeva,
O Rudra, Śaṅkara, Maheśvara,
O Śiva, Embodiment of the Mantra.

May you be glorified, O Fire of Śiva,
O Dreadful One, who,
Having absorbed the melting fat
Of the pieces of the three worlds,
Remain yet auspicious.

May the Lord be glorified,
The mysterious Śambhu
Whose only definition is that he is
Devoid of all definitions.

Glory to the imperceptible Lord,
The antithesis of the Vedas and the Āgamas
And yet the true essence
of the Vedas and the Āgamas.

Glory be to Śambhu,
The sole cause of the universe
And its only destroyer,
Who takes worldly form
And who transcends the world.

Glory be to Śambhu,
Who is the consummate beginning, middle, and end,
Who takes the form of beginning, middle, and end,
Who is without beginning, middle, or end.

The utterance of your name even once
Produces the same effect
As several virtuous deeds.
May you be glorified, O Difficult of Attainment.

Homage to the One who revels always
With a band of ghosts
In moving and in nonmoving forms.
May you be glorified, O Skullbearer,
O Essence of Consciousness.

Homage to that wondrous Śambhu,
The Deluding One
Who is yet pure and clear;
The Hidden One
Who has yet revealed himself;
The Subtle One
Whose form yet takes the form of the whole universe.

May you be glorified, O Omnipotent One,
Whose many acts bewilder,
Whose play is to destroy the world
Maintained by Brahmā, Indra, and Visnu.

May you be glorified, O Hara,
Fathomless ocean

On whose shores the mere wanderer
Acquires your special powers.

Homage to Śambhu, resplendent lotus
Dwelling unsullied
In the midst of the world's thick mire
Of illusion.

Homage to the Auspicious One,
The Pure, the Protector, the Adorned Soul,
The Beloved, the Highest Truth,
The Best of all things.

Homage to Śambhu,
The One who is ever bound
Yet enjoys eternal liberation:
Who is beyond bondage and liberation.

In this vast expanse of the three worlds,
Whose whole essence is ludicrous,
You are the sole enjoyer of perpetual delight.
May you be glorified, O One without a Second.

May you be glorified, O Śarva,
Who are the essence of the "righthanded" path,
Who are the essence of the "lefthanded" path,
Who claim every sect
And no sect at all.

May you be glorified, O Deva,
Who can be worshiped in any manner
In any place
In whatever form at all.

May you be glorified, O Granter of Boons,
Who are served by those aspiring for liberation,
And whose boundless depths of beauty
Dispel all afflictions.

May you be glorified, O Lord,
Who forever fill the three worlds
With infinite beatitude,
Rejoicing in eternal celebration.

Homage to your terrifying sense-goddesses!
Whatever they enjoy
Is all in offering to you.

May you be glorified, inaccessible
Even to the long-haired sages.
But those endowed with the spirit of devotion
Embrace you without difficulty.

May you be glorified,
Vessel of the sweetest nectar,
Treasury of supreme liberation,
Attainable far beyond the farthest limits.

May you be glorified, O Form of the Great *Mantra,*
Cool and lucid,
Blessed with exquisite fragrance,
Brimming with the great nectar of immortality.

The great cloth
Representing your absolute oneness
Is full of the nectar of freedom
And has not a single spot of color.
Homage to your teachings, O Lord.

We praise the path of Maheśvara,
The thunderbolt against all doubts,
The fire of destruction
That destroys all misfortune,
The final dissolution
Of all things inauspicious.

May you be glorified, O Deva!
Homage! Adoration!
O Protector of the Whole Universe,
O Supreme Lord of the Three Worlds,
For refuge I come to you alone.

STOTRA THREE

The Gift of Affection

Homage to the miraculous Śambhu, who,
Transcending the two forms—the real and the
    unreal—
Of all that exists,
Constitutes the Third Form.

In this threefold universe of bondage
The only ones who are free,
Including the gods and the sages,
Are those who arise from your freedom.

They enjoy perfect happiness
Who have the unique elixir
Against the ills of the world:
The remembrance that the entire universe
Is inlaid with your form.

Whose white canopy is the self-illumined moon,
Whose fly-whisk is the stream
Of the heavenly Gaṅgā—
He alone is the Supreme Lord.

Bestow on me your glance
Which radiates immortal nectar,
Cool and pure
Like a crescent of the moon.

Why, O Lord, do the drops of supreme knowledge
That flow from the ocean of your consciousness-bliss
Not have the delicious flavor
Of immortal sweetness?

Whose heart
Is not immersed in the delight of your nectar,
O Lord,
Has no heart at all.
O Mighty One! He should be despised!

Whose heart
Is united with you, O Lord,
Alone is worthy of Śambhu's powers.

Meditation on you
Washes away both delights and sorrows

As a river stream
Washes away high lands and low lands alike.

For those who feel no separation from you
And for whom you are dearer than their own souls—
What cannot be said
Of the abundance of their happiness!

I roar! Oh, and I dance!
My heart's desires are fulfilled
Now that you, Lord,
Infinitely splendid,
Have come to me.

In that state, O Lord,
Where nothing else is to be known or done,
Neither *yoga*
Nor intellectual understanding
Is to be sought after,
For the only thing that remains and flourishes
Is absolute consciousness.

Whose voice ever rings
With the eternal sound *Śiva*
Escapes spontaneously
The cruel grip of undefeatable, endless sorrows.

The "first person"
Is distinguished from the "second person"
And from the "third person" as well.
You alone are the Great Person,
The refuge of all persons.

O Lord of the Universe!
How lucky are your devotees,
Worthy of being adored by you.
For them, this turbulent ocean of the world
Is like a great pleasure-lake
For their amusement.

Those who delight in you
Long for nothing but to identify
With you completely.
How could worldly desires ever be requested!
For the devotees feel ashamed
Even in expressing the prayer:
"May you be revealed to me."

"Higher than Me there is nothing,
Yet even then I practice *japa*.
This shows that *japa* is but
Concentration on absolute oneness."

Thus you instruct your devotees
As well as the whole world
Through your *akṣamālā*.
In essence this is what constitutes *japa*.

The unreal is indeed different from the real,
And the real is indeed different from that, O Lord!
You are neither real nor unreal,
But the nature of real and unreal both.

Though you shine even more brilliantly
Than the rays of a thousand suns
And though you pervade all the worlds,
Still you are not visible.

In this unconscious world
You are the form of consciousness.
Among the knowable, you are the knower;
Among the finite, you are the infinite:
You are the highest of all.

"No more of these lamentations!"
I cry out loudly before the Lord,
For in spite of knowing all this
I am confused
And I stray from the right path.

STOTRA FOUR

Potent Nectar

You are to be praised, O my mind,
For even though you waver,
You worship the protector even of the protectors,
The *guru* of the three worlds,
The beloved of Ambikā.

Although I have gradually traversed
The steps of the various gods,
Having as support the feet of Śiva,
What a wonder it is that not even now
Do I part with this lowliest of states!

Show me the inner path!
Make disappear completely
The ways of the entire world
So that in an instant, O Lord,
I may become your servant forever.

O Śiva! Śiva! Śambhu! Śaṅkara!
O you who are kind to those seeking refuge,
Have mercy!
For blessings are not at all far away
From the memory of the pair of your lotus feet.

Lord! Reclining on the cushion of your lotus feet,
Those who create the world as they like
Laugh at Viriñci, who is subordinate
And who is completely smeared
With the soil of his own authority.

Nothing can shine that is separate
From the light of your form, O Lord.
Therefore, though disguised by nature,
You remain accessible.

Some people's perceptions become dulled
Because of duality.
But others taste immediately
The brilliant, unbroken body
That is free of duality.

O Lord, if that light of yours
Which is smeared with nectar
And which shines to me

Like infrequent flashes of lightning
Could be made more constant,
Then from that time my worship of you
Would also become constant
And nothing else would be required.

Just as here it is certain through great insight
That you are everything,
That there is nothing else
Either existent or nonexistent,
So, then, be abundantly evident to me!

By your own will, O Lord,
Have I set out on your path.
Why, then, do I behave like ordinary people
Instead of one worthy of you?

The sweetest emotion
Blossoms in the hearts of the *cātaka* birds
Who long enjoy that blissful experience
When they hear the rumblings of clouds.

Only through your grace
Has this enjoyment increased.
So even when the devotees
Are in a state of separation

Only the mention of you gives rise
To the remembrance of that joy of union.

He who utters the name of Śiva
Hundreds and hundreds of times
Grows great through the showering
Of the sweet, sublime nectar.
The marvelous power of this word
Enters even into the hearts of fools.

And that word, which flows like honey
From a nectar-crescent of the moon,
And causes the highest nectar to flow—
That is the sound of Śiva.
Blessed are they who have this sound
Ever on their lips.

This terrible world is about to be ended.
The deep stain of my mind has melted away.
Still the gates of your city
Are bolted shut
And do not unlatch even slightly.

Ardently I desire to behold
Your ever-blossoming lotus face.
O Lord, may you appear to me,

Howsoever faintly,
Face to face.

There is no other happiness here in this world
Than to be free of the thought
That I am different from you.
What other happiness is there?
How is it, then, that still this devotee of yours
Treads the wrong path?

If I do not continuously sip, with affection,
The wine of the nectar of harmony with you,
Then for a moment I will not be a fitting
Receptacle for your realization.

In truth, this person doesn't see
Even the slightest image of your form,
His mind sullied
By the sense of duality.
Even though you are omniscient
And show kindness to your followers
Why do you not hear this cry of mine?

Do you remember, O Lord,
That I ever sought after worldly pleasures
Or ever beseeched you for any of them?

Always greatly desired is the nectar
That comes from beholding your form.
That, oh grant me!

No sooner had I set foot
On the path of Śiva
Than, through your will,
Hundreds of auspicious things arose for me.
What else could I possibly ask of you, O Lord?

Where the sun, the moon, and all other stars
Set at the same time,
There rises the radiant Night of Śiva,
Spreading a splendor of its own.

O Lord of the Gods!
Without the taste of nectar from touching your feet,
Even gaining sovereignty in the three worlds
Holds for me no savor at all.

Alas, O Lord, this knot of the soul
Prevents your realization.
But fashioned and concealed by you,
That knot is strong indeed—
So strong that, disregarding you,
It slackens not a bit.

O Lord of the Gods!
You are an object of incessant worship
By the great ones,
But are yourself a worshiper.
Here in this world
You are an object of vision
From both within and without,
But are yourself a seer.

STOTRA FIVE

The Command of Powers

Carry me into your abode, O Lord—
I, who, through the touch of the *guru*
Have become attached
To the pleasure of the touch
Of your lotus feet.

The hair on my head glistens
With color from the dust of your lotus feet;
When shall I begin to dance
The dance of ever-impetuous delight?

O Lord! You are my only Lord!
I perpetually beseech
That I would sooner be made a mute
And dwell within you
Than become wise in any other way.

"O Lord! Ocean of Nectar!
O Gleaming Three-eyed One!
O Sweet One even of the Monstrous Eyes!"
Let me cry and dance
Exclaiming all this with joy.

With my eyes closed
At the touch of your lotus feet,
May I rejoice,
Reeling with drunkenness
From the wine of your devotion.

May I dwell somewhere in a glen
Of the mountain of your consciousness
Where lies the uninterrupted state
Of your sublime bliss.

May I live in that sanctuary, O Lord,
Where, taking many forms,
You reside with Devī
From the palace up to the city gates.

O Lord, may the rays
Of your brilliance beam steadily
Until the lotus of my heart opens
To worship you.

Grant, O Lord,
That I fall at your feet always
And find such delight there
That even my mind becomes intoxicated
And dissolves in bliss.

Whether through immense joy or through anguish,
Whether from on a wall or in an earthen jug,
Whether from external objects or from within,
Reveal yourself to me, O Lord!

So cool is the nectar
From the touch of your lotus feet!
May that always stream through me,
Within and without.

Plunging into the ambrosia-lake
Of touching your feet
Is ever for me a pleasure
Beyond all pleasures.

Accept false enjoyment and the other limitations
That I offer unto you, O Lord.
Having transformed them into immortal nectar,
Enjoy them together with the devotees.

Contented with your meal
Of the entire world,
Be comfortably seated;
Then bestow on us, your devotees,
Your blessings and your blissful glance.

With my eyes closed,
Relishing the wonder of inner devotion,
May l worship even the blades of grass thus:
"Homage to Śiva, my own consciousness!"

Having seen the world as consisting of your nature
And having realized the pleasure
Of your nondual form,
Still may I never part
With the enjoyment of the spirit of devotion.

O Lord, since you and you alone
Have no wish that is unfulfilled,
Then the fulfillment of your nonduality
Is more than sufficient.

May I attain that state
Where one laughs, one dances,
One does away with passion and hatred
And other such things,

And where one drinks
Of the sweet nectar of devotion.

May the extraordinary fragrance
Of the blossom of your remembrance
Become fixed in my heart
Until the stench of foul impressions fades away.

O Lord, enlighten my heart!
Help me to discriminate between
The base delight in false enjoyments
And the superior delight in your lotus feet.

Although I roam about in the states of *yoga*
And am not caught up in worldly affairs,
I would rather that my heart tremble,
Intoxicated with the wine of your remembrance.

In speech, in thought,
In the perceptions of the mind,
And in the gestures of the body,
May the sentiment of devotion be my companion
At all times, in all places.

Śiva! Śiva! Śiva!
Thus is performed the worship
Of constantly repeating your name.

O Lord, may I continue to taste the sweetest nectar,
Which is never repetitious.

May I live, worshiping you
In the world made of
Pulsating, endless, consciousness,
Along the path where
All unconsciousness has been dispelled,
In the city made of
Your unfathomable, extraordinary consciousness.

"Nothing at all is of use
For becoming firmly established, shining manifest,
Eternally in one's own form."
May this thought take deep root in me,
Purified by the dust of your lotus feet.

When I touch the soles of your feet,
It sometimes flashes in my mind
That this whole world
Has merged into a lake of nectar.
Lord! Grant this to me always!

STOTRA SIX

Tremblings along the Journey

Separated from you
Even for an instant, O Lord,
I suffer deeply.
May you always be the subject of my sight.

Even if I am separated
From the world of *saṃsāra*
May I not be separated from you,
My beloved.

Wherever I go with body, speech, and mind,
Everything that there is, is you alone.
May this highest truth indeed
Become perfectly realized within me.

O Lord! Offering you prayers,
May my speech become just as you are:

Beyond all distinctions
And filled with the highest bliss.

From the experience of union with you
Let me wander about
Free of every need and desire
Filled with absolute joy
Seeing all of creation as you alone.

O Lord, may l perceive the whole world
As filled with you
So much so that I, too,
Be completely satisfied:
Then, no longer will you be bothered
With my entreaties.

Just as cloud droplets are absorbed in the sky,
So are the various constituents of the universe
Absorbed in you;
May they always shine visibly for me
As I proceed through the stages
Of spiritual growth.

From the center of the world
Let there be visible to me
Your magnificent jewel

That dispells the depths of darkness
With its radiant luster.

On what site do you not dwell?
What exists that does not exist in your body?
I am wearied!
Therefore let me reach you everywhere,
Without difficulty.

O Lord, may I realize at will
The bliss of embracing your form.
Having attained that,
What have I not accomplished!

Be visible, O Lord!
We do not trouble you with other requests.
Anguished, we chase after you.

STOTRA SEVEN

Victory over Separation

Having found harmony in your sea of bliss
May my heart be rid of this sorry state
Of disharmony
Once and for all.

May the axe of faith
In the oneness of your form
Fall on the firm root
Of false attachments, hatred,
And the other bonds that become manifest as
"This is mine, this is not mine."

O Lord, may the chain of the stigmas
Of contradictions perish.
May absolute freedom flash forth in my heart.
May the image made of consciousness
Be flooded with the nectar of bliss.

I toss within the egg
Of the world infested with false attachments.
Like a mother, may the devotional sentiment
Nourish me with the sweet essence of bliss
So that I may develop into a bird
With mighty wings.

Acquiring the skill to taste the sweet nectar
Derived from worshiping your feet,
May these longings of my mind
For the poison of sense objects
Be destroyed in their entirety.

Having been touched
By the sunbeams of your devotion,
Let this heart-crystal of mine
Shoot forth the blazing sparks of the passions,
Eradicating them completely.

Forever may I sing my praises
Loudly to you,
Located in that place where Hari,
Haryaśva, and Viriñca are waiting outside.

With the restless joy
Born of the rapture of devotion

May I perceive, entirely through the senses,
The whole world in the form of Śiva
And every action to consist of worship.

May my mind be wedded to devotion,
And through that union
May children be born
In the form of *aṇimā* and the other powers.
May they mature
So as to strengthen my feeling that
"All these are mine."

STOTRA EIGHT

Unearthly Strength

When will that small amount of grace
Abiding with the Lord
And that small amount of devotion
That has come to me
Unite to become like that unique form——
The blissful body of Śiva?

Here in this world
May there arise in me continually
The blissful experience of the highest fulfillment
That comes from your supremacy.
May *jñāna, yoga,* and powers such as *aṇimā*
Remain afar.

Let me, like other people,
Yearn deeply for the objects of the world,

But allow me to view them as your form,
O Lord, without contradiction.

In the different stages
Of the growth of the body,
In the modifications of the mind,
In the many situations
On the path of life,
Reveal to me your own blissful form.

Let the sense faculties, full of delight,
Be attached to their respective objects.
But may there not be, even for an instant,
Any loss of the joy
Of your nonduality.

As I become absorbed within you,
Experiencing your form—so light,
Mild, clear, and cool—
May I transcend that behavior of ordinary life
Dependent upon material objects.

May my body blossom into your true nature,
The worlds become my limbs.
May all this dualistic feeling

Be forgotten forever,
Even after crossing into the realm of memory.

From the vision of your face
May there arise for me
A flood of the highest nectar
So that the terrible cavern
Obscuring my realization of your form
Be filled in completely.

Whenever I am sprinkled with even a few drops
Of the nectar of your touch
I become indifferent to
All the pleasures of the world.
Why must I be deprived of both types of pleasures?

O Unborn One!
May I, the royal swan perpetually gliding
Across the lake of your lotus feet,
Reach the top, middle, and indeed the root
Of the lotus stalk of devotion.

May there exist, O Lord,
All the objects of my thought and my sight.
But may each of them blossom

As the bliss of vision, reflection,
And illumination.

O Mightiest Lord!
Even when there is a deluge of those miseries
May I not only be free from fear,
But may I also enjoy the blissful, supreme
Exultation at the touch of your body.

While woven into your being
This entire universe
Is also projected outward.
I have come to understand this
Through strong determination;
May I realize it also
Through sensual experience.

STOTRA NINE

The Triumph of Freedom

When shall my heart, anxiously longing
For a new experience of tender devotion,
Abandon all else
And come to touch you?

Of you alone enamored,
Having as my only treasure
The worship of your feet,
When shall I make you visible, O Lord,
Before these very eyes?

When shall my mind
Indifferent to all else through love's intensity
Tear open the great door latch
With a loud bang
And finally arrive in your presence, O Lord?

Through the power of your devotion, O Lord,
When shall I overcome all of the gods
Who reside in my heart,
The core of consciousness?

When shall I enjoy the bounteous celebration
Of the rapture of devotion,
Where the elements of the objective world
Become filled with the bliss of consciousness?

When shall that moment come, O Lord,
When all of a sudden I recognize you,
The Fearless, Exalted, Whole, Without Cause,
The One, indeed, to have veiled himself—
And in so doing make you ashamed?

When, O Lord, shall I become
Such a cherished devotee of yours
That you never consider it appropriate
To run away from me?

Viewing all creatures as immersed in your worship—
When shall I retain this vision,
And be flooded with its sweet, delightful nectar?

When shall my yearning for devotion—
The highest state of knowledge and

The highest stage of *yoga*—
Become fulfilled, O Lord?

When shall I become helplessly enraptured
And reveal to everyone my joy,
Having suddenly obtained and firmly clasped
The treasure of your most precious feet?

When, O Lord, shall I possess
Your pure, far-reaching radiance
So that never may I become sullied
By the shadow of *māyā*?

Having assimilated into myself this orb of the world,
And free of all desires,
When, O Lord, shall I become prominent
In the community of your devotees?

Of the pride in the world,
You are the one cause.
Bursting with the spirit of your devotion,
When shall I attain the Great Pride?

Replete with all objects, embraced by Śrī,
When shall I comfortably take my rest
At the pair of your soothing lotus feet?

When shall I, flushed with the wine of devotion,
Reach the limits of joy in your worship,
Attaining the highest fulfillment, O Lord?

When shall I have the bliss of your touch
So that I stammer and lose my voice,
Choking on streams of blissful tears,
With peals of laughter abloom on my face?

When, O Lord, shall I shake off
This habit of acting like brutish people
So that I enjoy an attitude
Befitting your devotees?

Having attained *aṇimā* and the other powers
And having overcome all fears of distress,
When shall I lose myself in the pastime
Of drinking that magical, life-giving draft?

When, O Lord, shall my voice
Produce such a lament
That your image flashes suddenly before my eyes?

With my heart set on
Tightly embracing your lotus feet,
When shall I behold you without any effort
In the form of being and nonbeing both?

STOTRA TEN

Breaking the Continuity

Surely you, the sole presiding deity of the universe,
Should not tolerate the followers of Maheśvara
Behaving like the ordinary people of the world.

Those who, through never-ending affection
Have become the followers of your feet,
Derive the deepest pleasures
From anything that they do.

Where you, the Great Destroyer, are protector,
How can there be any disease?
Wherever your Lakṣmī resides,
What other desire for enjoyment can there be?

Whoever should obtain the all-pervading Lord
For just a moment's happiness

Becomes filled with your bliss for all time,
Even from that very instant.

The moon is a drop of the nectar of your bliss
That has trickled down to earth,
Just as the sun is a mere particle
Of your brilliant light, O Lord.

We dedicate ourselves to this,
Your third eye,
The one symbol of your transcendental mystery.

Who is much exalted, beholding you
Has truly your realization.
Who is struck suddenly with ineffable joy—
He too has your realization.

Having gotten into your heart, O Lord,
Those granted with your grace
Have withdrawn the exterior world from you
And merged it within the interior.

Everything else except you, O Lord,
Has two eyes—that is, even—eyes.
But you, the only Lord of the world,
Are of the uneven eyes.

Without you, your opponents
Would not be able to speak ill of you.
Even their disparaging remarks
Would not exist but through your majesty.

If, O Lord, there be in my heart
A place for you that is free
Of inner and outer obstacles—
What else then would be needed?

Some wander about from birth to birth,
Utterly restless souls.
Others, Lord, move throughout the world,
Joyously equipoised.

Without having drunk of the nectar of your devotion
And without having beheld your essence,
Even then do people become perfected
By merely hearing about you, O Lord.

We are your servants, O Lord!
Therefore we should receive the same care from you
As you foster on the soul of the three worlds.

Having seen you, the soul of the world,
Made of the nectar of the highest bliss,

Even now do I yet more intensely
Long for the ecstacy of your touch.

All misfortunes suffered by those of the world
Become tolerable
When joined with that form of yours
Known as constancy.

With you existing as the essence of consciousness,
Omniscient and omnipotent,
The manifestation of this world—
Appearing as false in every respect—
Is understood as your true form.

Enlivened by you, these senses quiver
Though they be like lumps of clay.
They dance, like feathery fluffs of cotton
Raised up by the breeze.

If, O Lord, the senses were not
Endowed with self-consciousness,
Then who would forsake the realization
That the world is one with you?

They are to be praised, O Supreme Lord,
Who, while yet in the state of dissolution

Have been purified
By the touch of the fire of your wrath.

Though you stand completely manifest
With a body of splendrous light,
Why do I wander about, O Lord,
In darkness?

You, the indivisible Lord, are my immortal form.
Yet still, I am only an abode
Of mortal characteristics.

Whose speech is adorned
With the name *Maheśvara*
And whose forehead bears the mark
Of salutation,
Is indeed alone the exalted one.

Since you indeed are real and unreal
Why then do I not realize you
Without any effort,
Spontaneously?

For a servant of Śiva
Who has identified himself with Śiva,
What happiness is there that cannot be attained?

Therefore even the heads of the gods
Serve me the wine of immortality.

Between the heart and the navel of living beings,
In the form of the great digestive fire
You devour all
That moves and moves not.

STOTRA ELEVEN

Bound to the World by Desire

Neither this world
Nor a friend
Nor a relative
Belongs to me at all.
When you are all this
Who else then could be mine?

You, O Master, are the Great Lord.
You are in truth the entire world.
Thus, asking for any one specific thing
Is just the asking
And nothing more.

Supremacy over the three worlds appears
As trifling as a piece of straw
To those who are devoted to you.

What other fruit than your remembrance
Need their good deeds bear?

When nothing at all is different from you
And even the creator of the worlds
Is your creation,
There is no need, then, to sing the praises
Of your miraculous deeds.

I am one with you,
Constantly immersed in worshiping you.
Since I am like this all the time,
Why can I not realize it naturally
Even when I am dreaming?

Those who have gotten just a whiff
Of the fragrance, however slight,
Of your lotus feet—
To them all things of enjoyment,
Even those much desired by the gods,
Appear putrid.

It isn't the case
That there is one thing in your heart,
Another in your speech,
And yet another in your actions.

Be clear, O Śambhu!
Bestow either grace or punishment.

I am confused, overcome with sorrow.
Old age and infirmities terrify me.
My strength gone, I come to you for shelter.
Therefore, grant, O Śambhu, that before long
The highest of all states be reached by me,
Far beyond the path of pain.

When they reach your ears
My laments, however meager,
Become precious
Like the drops of rain
That one by one,
Falling in the core of the bamboo shoot,
Become pearls.

What, O Lord, is not attained
By those people who even for a moment pretend
To be devoted to your name?
O bearer of the crescent moon on your head,
Allow that, vanquishing death,
I may attain *aṇimā* and the other powers.

O Śambhu, O Śarva,
Bearer of the crescent moon on your head,
O Śiva, O Three-eyed One,
Bearer of the Prayer Beads, O Venerable One,
Having Horrifying Skulls as your Symbol,
O Brilliant One,
Having Fearsome Trident as your Weapon,
O Ocean of Compassion, O Ferocious Power,
Creator of the Three Worlds, O Śrīkaṇṭha!
Quickly annihilate all of this inauspiciousness
And bestow on me the highest perfection.

What, O Master, could exist,
Whose creator is not the Lord?
What does a sentient being experience
That is not due to the great, immutable
Powers of Śaṅkara?
I ever abide in you,
But even so I am constantly depressed,
Struggling with mental agonies.

O Granter of Boons, here in this world
Inevitable are pain, old age, and death.
But leave these aside for a moment:
Even the highly esteemed Sound itself
And other such things are ephemeral.

Even so, I long for everlasting happiness,
For the enduring, eternal elixir of life——
The sweet meditation on your lotus feet.

O Master, expert at vanquishing
The miseries of devotees,
Treasure of auspiciousness,
Having matted locks——
Now, when I am an abode only of pain,
Grant me the highest perfection of your worship
While I am still living
And fit for the sweetest of pleasures.

May he be glorified
Whose eternal activity
Is the destruction of the great veil of illusion,
Whose symbol is the moon,
Whose light outshines all other lights.

STOTRA TWELVE

Particulars of the Arcane Lore

Everything is saturated with you alone.
Why, when this is the case, O Lord,
Do you not reveal yourself,
Even now?

You are dominant
In worldly objects,
In the various sense organs,
And when I am enlightened with knowledge.
Even while you permeate all of these things
You are beyond them.
May I have that revelation at all times.

Those who proceed on the path of beholding you
Are fortunate to have your blessings.
How can they be reborn
And how can they be known by anyone?

They are decorated
With the naturally glorious symbol.
You lift them up again and again
From ordinary things in their worldly life——
From water, from grass, and from other things——
And you fill them with waves of nectar.

Satiated with the nectar
Flowing from the direct realization of your form,
Having eradicated desire,
Intoxicated,
They wander about at their will.

Neither "then" nor "always"
Nor even "once."
Where no perception of time exists,
That very thing is your realization.
And it can neither be called eternal nor anything else.

With my heart pining for your vision
May I only attain this much power through *yoga*:
That by merely wishing it
I may gain entrance to the innermost sanctuary
To perform your worship.

With minds blossomed
From attaining an unwavering vision of you,

The actions and words of devotees
Are flawless—naturally.

O Lord, may my permanent abode
Be at your feet
And may I be fearless.
Whatever my station in the world
May I worship you
With actions unrestricted.

Having completely entered
Your lotus feet,
Having lost all desires,
Let me consume the most bounteous honey
And wander about at will,
Completely satisfied.

Even for him whose thought of worshiping you
Arises only hypocritically,
Inevitably he acquires an appropriate
Closeness to you.

O Lord, indifferent to everything else,
With only one delight in my heart,
Shall I ever drink enough of the Lord,
Who is easily accessible,
Who is all-calming?

Separated from you,
All this, whatever it may be,
Should be rejected.
And everything consisting of you
Should be accepted.
This, in short, is the essence
(Of all spiritual wisdom).

The objective world,
Moving about within you,
Is to be adored.
So then, outside of you, Lord,
How can nonexistence be conceived of,
Much less adored?

O Three-eyed One!
Transcending speech and empirical knowledge,
Let me, without obstacles,
Behold only you, Lord,
Everywhere, all the time,
Even when emotionally agitated.

Reveal, O Deva, your abode
Where you ever reside with Parameśvarī.
Those who abide

In the midst of the dust of the Master's feet—
Are such servants unreliable?

Even having come along
On the path of seeing you,
Why, my Lord, do you elude your servant?
For what creature here on earth
Do you not present yourself for a moment?

Inundated with the pure,
Endlessly flowing stream of nectar
Of the supreme knowledge
That all is one,
When, O Lord, shall I realize absolute identification
Between you and my physical form,
And obtain never-ending bliss?

So that I may become your worshiper,
Let me attain just the smallest share
Of the essence of that insight
Into how the world becomes bound up in misery.

Every moment, while beholding different objects,
Let me clearly see you and you alone, O Lord,
As assuming the form of the whole universe.

Why does my mind not view
The various objects of my desire
As not different from the limbs of your body?
In so doing, it would not lose its nature
And my highest desire would also be realized.

Hundreds indeed are those, O Lord,
Who through your inspiration
While living the lives of average people
Perceive just through these very eyes
Your form ever before them.

Not a thought arises
That does not constitute your will.
All acts, favorable or otherwise,
Are always performed by the Lord himself.
Thus abiding in you, I wander through the world
With nothing to frustrate the festival
Of the worship of your spotless feet.

May insight into your mysterious language
Dawn on me completely.
May I develop such power
That worshiping you incessantly
Becomes a habit.

Let even my various worldly concerns
Always appear to me thus:
As part of you, and therefore not worthy
In and of themselves.

While my mind wanders of its own inclinations
Here and there in the range of the senses,
Let me become in your worship, O Lord,
An adept unwavering.

Through your will alone was I born your servant—
Through no other force.
Even then, why am I never blessed
With the vision of your countenance?
How strange!

Those who long for you intensely
Discover you in every object.
Oh, what spiritual path do they follow
That has yielded them this fruit?

May all objects, Your Majesty,
Appear to me as truly embodying your being.
Let nothing else
Mean a thing to me.

Whatever is not,
Let that be nothing to me.
Whatever is,
Let that be something to me.
In this way may it be
That you be found and worshiped by me
In all states.

STOTRA THIRTEEN

In Summary . . .

Hear in summary, O Lord,
What defines my joy and my sorrow:
Union with you is joyousness;
Separation, deep agony.

There is, within me,
The tiniest dark spot
That keeps you hidden.
Completely wiping away even that,
Reveal, O Lord, your spotless form.

In whatever state of being—
Life, death, or anything else—
May I worship you constantly
In your imperishable body
That embraces the whole world
And consists of the bliss of eternal consciousness.

I am the Lord.
I, indeed, am the Handsome One,
The Learned One, the Fortunate.
Who else is there in the world
Like me?
Such a splendid feeling
Befits only your devotees.

Therefore with the consciousness
Of the true essence of things
That emanates from the removal of
The obstacles to the nectar of your nonduality,
Make me worthy, O Lord of the Gods,
Of the worship of your feet.

Let there be that great festival of worship
Where the Supreme Lord himself
Is meditated upon, seen, and touched.
Be always mine through your grace.

The realization of things as they really are
And the supreme festival of your worship—
One is intertwined with the other,
And they always blossom
In those who are filled with devotion.

While incessantly drinking in through the senses
The heady wine of your worship
From the overflowing goblets of all objects,
Let madness overtake me.

Where not even a trace
Of otherness exists,
Where self-luminosity is everywhere manifest,
There, in your city,
Let me reside
Forever as your worshiper.

It is by your own will, O Supreme Lord,
That I hold a position as your servant.
Why, then, am I not deserving to behold you
Or even of the task of pressing your feet?

Lord, although it is fitting,
You never discriminate
When bestowing grace.
What has befallen me now that you delay
In revealing a glimpse of yourself?

Worshiping you with my own hands,
Let me behold you, together with Parameśvarī,
Shining in all things exterior and interior,
Ever filling the three worlds.

Having ascended to the Master's palace
By sheer intent,
Without obstruction,
Let me always enjoy the sweetest bliss
Of drinking the immortal wine of your grace.

That which bestows on all objects of beauty
The property of giving wonder at the mere touch—
By that very principle do those endowed with
Unwavering devotion
Worship your form.

Being self-luminous
You cause everything to shine;
Delighting in your form
You fill the universe with delight;
Rocking with your own bliss
You make the whole world dance with joy.

He who without hesitation
Views all of this tangible world as your form,
Having filled the universe
With the form of his own self,
Is eternally joyful.
Why, then, the fear?

Even the deadly poison
That rests in a corner of your throat, O Lord,
Is supreme nectar to me.
Nectar that is separate from your body,
Even if easily accessible,
Doesn't interest me.

May my countenance be ever flushed with excitement
From talking and singing about you.
And may I ever be blessed with the desire
To perform your worship of love.

Oh, the ways of the Supreme Lord
Cannot be reckoned!
He has presented me his own being,
Bursting with sweet, immortal nectar,
But yet does not allow me
To drink.

Entering you, my own being,
The fathomless, the undifferentiated,
The one without a second,
Devouring all sense of (subject and) object,
O Lord of Umā,
Ever may I worship and sing praises of you.

STOTRA FOURTEEN

Song of Glorification

In the presence of my Master,
Repository of the most magnificent wealth,
Let me relish the nectar
Of chanting glorifications again and again.

May you be glorified, the one Rudra,
The one Śiva, the Great God, The Great Lord,
Beloved of Pārvatī,
Firstborn of All the Gods.

May you be glorified, Lord of the Three Worlds,
Bearing on your forehead the unique third eye.
May you be glorified, who bear on your throat
The mark of deadly poison,
Having swallowed the afflictions of the afflicted.

May you be glorified, in whose hand glistens
The sharp trident symbolic of the three powers.
May you be glorified,
Whose most venerable lotus feet
Can fulfill a desire the moment it arises.

May you be glorified, whose transcendental form
Radiates manifold splendor.
May you be glorified, whose forehead bears ashes
And in a single tuft of whose hair
Flows the stream of Gaṅgā.

May you be glorified, anointed with moonlight
Reflected in the vast ocean of milk.
May you be glorified, O Lord whose ornaments
Are snakes dazzling with jewels
Begotten at your touch.

May you be glorified, O worthy refuge
Of the only immortal crescent of the moon.
May you be glorified, ever consecrated
As the lord of the universe
With the waters of Gaṅgā.

May you be glorified, the mere touch of whose feet
Has made sacred the entire bovine family.

May you be glorified, who always appear
At the gatherings of devotees.

May you be glorified, who through your own will
Deceive fools by assuming ascetic disguise.
May you be glorified, who enjoy the deserved
Propitious fortune of Gaurī's embrace.

May you be glorified, who delight in offerings
Drenched in the sentiment of devotion.
May you be glorified, pleased with the singing
And dancing of devotees drunk on your wine.

May you be glorified, who bring about
The birth and death of the powers
Of Brahmā and the other lords of the gods.
May you be glorified, whose orders are carried out
By the ranks of the lords of the universe.

May you be glorified,
Who have made manifest your grandeur
By placing your signet
On each and every thing in the world.
May you be glorified, Great Lord,
Lord of the universe into which
You have infused your own soul.

May you be glorified, who are without second
When the will arises to create the three worlds.
May you be glorified, whose only assistant is
Devī, treasury of all of your powers.

May you be glorified, who permeate
All the three worlds simultaneously.
May you be glorified, whose sound, *Īśvara*,
Is never despised, not even by fools.

May you be glorified, whose innate supremacy
Depends neither on compassion nor other virtues.
May you be glorified, whose unique, destructive
    powers
Destroy even the Great Death.

May you be glorified, unobstructed
In bringing about universal annihilation.
May you be glorified, the chanting of whose name
Is followed by a thousand auspicious qualities.

May you be glorified, who without the slightest
    effort
Gave away this ocean of nectar.
May you be glorified, a moment of whose wrath
Sets the universe in flames.

May you be glorified,
The only lamp for worldly beings
Blinded by the darkness of delusion.
May you be glorified, O Supreme Person,
Ever awake in the midst of a sleeping world.

May you be glorified, a partridge warbling
Within the mountain grove of my body.
May you be glorified, most excellent swan
Gliding through the skies
Of the minds of devotees.

May you be glorified, lord of the
Mountain of gold and other precious metals.
May you be glorified, an inauspicious moon
That descends like a meteor
Upon those who defy you.

May you be glorified, difficult of attainment
For ascetics and gods pained by harsh austerities.
May you be glorified, easily attainable
By the community of devotees in every state.

May you be glorified, who have
Made worthy of a stream of fortunes
Those who seek refuge in you.

May you be glorified, whose only purpose
Is to care lovingly for
Those who have come to you.

May you be glorified, outstanding
As the one causative factor in the creation,
Preservation, and destruction of the world.
May you be glorified, O great joy of Utpala,
Whose work is rendered as sheer delight
Through the madness of devotion.

May you be glorified, O Worthy of Devotion!
May you be glorified,
Conqueror of birth, old age, and death.
May you be glorified, O World Patriarch!
Glory, glory, glory, glory,
Glory, glory, glory, glory,
Glory, glory, glory, glory,
Glory, O Three-eyed Lord!

STOTRA FIFTEEN

About Devotion

There are scriptures that can cleanse a person
Of the three impurities.
And there are those yogins and pandits
Who have mastered these scriptures.
But the only ones truly equipoised
Are those devoted to you.

Well satisfied with the food
Of *kāla, niyati, rāga,* and
The other coverings of *māyā,*
The devotees wander joyfully, O Lord,
Along the shores of the world.

Whether weeping or laughing, they address you
In loud, delirious speech.
Uttering hymns of praise, the devoted
Are truly unique attendants.

My wish is to be neither an ascetic
Indifferent to the world
Nor a manipulator of supernatural powers
Nor even a worshiper craving liberation—
But only to become drunk
On the abundant wine of devotion.

I bow to him who,
Drawing the outside world into his heart,
Worships you, O Lord,
With streams of the nectar of devotion.

Amidst righteousness and unrighteousness,
Amidst works and knowledge,
Amidst prosperity and hardship,
Your devotees, in the face of all this,
Enjoy the bliss of your devotion.

O Master, father of the mobile and immobile,
Even the blind and the leprous
Look exceedingly graceful
When adorned with your supreme devotion.

O Lord, those who are filled
With the great warmth of devotion,
Although pale in body,

And having husks of grain as a bed
And as clothing the feathers of birds,
Dominate even over the Lord of Wealth.

As they ascend to you
Rolling, immersed in the nectar of your devotion,
A few, O Lord, worship you
With their whole being
Through their hearts.

O Lord, it is worthy of
Protection, support, and high esteem—
This great wealth of your devotion,
Which removes the troubles of the world.

Although your community of devotees, Lord,
Is passionately attached to you,
May Svāminī, leaving envy behind,
Be ever pleased with them.

Once there is devotion to you,
Union with you is certain.
Once a large pitcher of milk has been obtained,
Vain is a concern about yogurt.

Is this not an unparalleled *siddhi*;
Does it not cause supreme bliss to flow?—

This increasing devotion to Śambhu
That becomes everlasting.

Alas, submerged in my darkened mind
The exquisite jewel of your devotion
Does not manifest the innate, sublime
Flashes of its own splendor.

Devotion to you, Master of the Three Worlds,
Is indeed the supreme *siddhi*.
But without *aṇimā* and the other powers,
Even that, O Lord, is not perfect.
This is my anguish.

Emitting the sweet fragrance of *Śiva* flowers,
Which blossom within and without,
The yogins perfume even those of ill habits
Who come into their presence.

Where not even the notion of light exists,
Where the whole world remains asleep,
There, in that state of Śivarātri,
The devotees, without pause, O Lord,
Honor you in worship.

Let *sattva* shine forth in the worship of Śiva,
Lord of the True Qualities.
Let heaps of dust from Lord Śaṅkara's feet
Shine as *rajas* on my head.
Let *tamas* flourish and completely destroy
The impressions of memory and the other
    attachments.
Thus, Lord, may the three *guṇa*s as a unit
Merge together with your being.

Endless is the cycle of birth and death.
These slender limbs are consumed
By diseases harsh and diverse.
I have derived no real enjoyment
From pleasures of the senses.
What happiness encountered was not long lasting.
Thus, my existence has become useless.
Grant me, O Lord,
Those sublime and everlasting treasures
So that I may become your devotee
With my head illumined by touching the feet
Of the One adorned with the moon.

STOTRA SIXTEEN

Breaking out of the Fetters

What indeed is there in the world
That does not conceal you?
Yet nothing exists that can conceal
You from the devotees.

Attained by so many disciples
And with so many attributes
You appear at all times to the devotees
In your true form, O Lord.

Triumphant, they laugh,
And vanquished, they laugh even more—
Those select few who are maddened
With the immortal wine of your devotion.

Let me delight in the sweet, sublime
Bliss of your devotion,

Leaving behind not only base powers,
But liberation itself.

In the same way that it arose in me,
Allow this love of devotion
Previously unknown to me
To grow greater still, O Lord.

Truly, I have no other entreaty but this:
Let me for all time, O Lord,
Be consumed with unending devotion.

Let me be enraged and yet
Compassionate toward the world.
And thus in the madness of devotion
May I laugh and weep and chant
Śiva, thunderously.

Under the spell of devotion, O Lord,
Let me be inconstant yet at peace,
Mournful yet laughing,
Distracted yet aware.

Whether within or without,
Your devotees know you
As the embodiment of consciousness.

Though pretending to listen
To the words of blasphemers,
And with needle-like sensations prickling the skin,
Enraptured still are the devotees
With drops of delicious nectar.

However painful a sensation,
It is transformed into a means of enjoyment
For devotees whose consciousness
Is suffused with the moonlight nectar.

Living in whatever state,
The devotees enjoy—both within and without—
The sublime bliss
Of the touch of your being.

A chosen few, O Lord, surpass
Plaintiveness when worshiping you,
And enjoy your spotless, immortal form.

The knowers of *śāstra*s become deluded
And thus become estranged:
Indeed, delusion produces estrangement.
But you appear for devotees
As the one, unrivaled truth.

How can he be like other people—
The devotee with mind made pure
By exhausting fame and infamy,
Attachment and aversion?

What position do the followers
Of the path of knowledge
Hold over these great souls
Who have vanquished the gloom of attachment and
     aversion
With the bright light of your devotion?

Whose worship consists
Of bathing in and drinking of
The nectar of devotion
Finds rest in the transcendental peace
Of the first, middle, and last stages.

You alone are the subject
Of their songs and speculations,
You, the subject of their quests and their worship.
Laudable, then, is the devotee's pilgrimage of life
Lived in harmony with you.

What is called liberation
Is simply the maturity of devotion, O Lord.

Having taken the first steps toward that,
We are even now almost liberated.

With my mind spilling over with your devotion,
Let any difficulty come my way.
But should I feel separate from you,
I would not want
Even an endless chain of happiness.

You are pleased, O Lord, with devotion.
And devotion arises at your will.
You alone understand
How these are connected.

Having a form or formless,
Within or without,
In every way, O Lord,
You are the embodiment of immortality
For those who are drunk with your devotion.

Here in this world
Another world exists
That bears as fruit joyousness
For your devotees.

May there be devotion to you
As the Secret One, as the Transcendent One,

As Lord of the Universe,
As Śambhu, as Śiva,
As the Celestial One,
Ah, how indeed could I ever express it?

Devotion, devotion, devotion
To the Transcendent One.
Ardent devotion!
This is why I cry and clamor!
Let me have ardent devotion for you,
Only you.

You are the fountainhead, O Lord,
Of everything beautiful.
All things become precious at your touch,
Whether gem or piece of straw.

Not separating themselves from you
When experiencing, through the senses,
The subject and object—
They indeed are your true devotees.

Some, O Lord, embrace you
Outside of world society.
Others forego all the rules,
And through the warmth of devotion
Embrace you in the midst of the world.

I honor Śiva, who
During the festival of the world's dissolution
Is passionately and intensely held by Śivā,
Through whom the whole universe is enjoyed
By means of drinking, eating, and embellishments.

O Lord of the Universe,
Glorious is your sovereignty!
Similarly glorious is your other state,
Where the world appears
Not as it appears here and now.

STOTRA SEVENTEEN

A High Regard for Divine Amusements

Ah, most glorious
Is this blissful festival of worship
From which spring tears
Of the sweet nectar of immortality.

All actions connected with your worship
Will promote *siddhis*.
But for your devotees
Who are already one with you,
These actions are *siddhis* in and of themselves.

Those who in every state worship you always
As having assumed the form of all things—
They indeed
Are my chosen deities.

The *siddha* leaves behind the effort of meditation,
For all of his joy is obtained from your touch.
That, O Lord, for the devotees
Comprises an act of worship.

The time of the equinox,
Whose essence is equanimity,
Is celebrated by the devotees continuously:
For always does their worship consist
Of the sweet bliss of your devotion.

Without a beginning, without an end,
And unlimited by time—
This is the essence of worship, O Lord,
Performed only by devotees.

They are the lords
Even over Brahmā and the other gods,
And they are the recipients of auspiciousness—
Those in whom the festival of worship
Stays constant even while dreaming
And indeed even in dreamless sleep.

Devotees celebrate the festival of worship
Not only while performing *japa*,
Pouring oblations into the fire,

Bathing, or meditating—
But in all states.

Who among the leading gods—
Indra, Brahmā, and the others—
And even among ascetics,
Is equal to the one who enjoys
The sweet nectar of your worship?

In the great festival of your worship
The devotees attain the attainable:
The sole cause of the world's annihilation.
This they understand indeed.

Resting in the brilliance of your consciousness,
May I ever worship you, O Lord,
By means of body, speech, and mind,
The products of the thirty-six *tattva*s.

Contented, enjoying attachment to your worship,
May all of my time become endless.
Only for this
Is it that I pray.

May my yearning for the enjoyment
Of the immortal bliss of your worship

Grow greater each day,
Ever yielding a bounteous harvest.

In your ocean brimming over
With the immortal bliss of unity
Cast outward at the dissolution of the universe,
May I there remain, O Great Soul, ever adoring you.

Having become pure and uncomplicated
By cutting through the knots of latent desires,
The devotees can finally dedicate their minds
To the sweet act of your worship.

Even while resting on their objects
The faculties of these senses provide
The devotees with the immortal wine
Essential to your worship, O Lord.

For devotees irresistably inflamed
With the burning heat of ardent devotion,
What other means of extinguishment are needed
Than plunging into the nectar of your worship?

May I experience the endless joy, O Lord,
Of drinking the nectar of the worship of your feet:
The only means to receive your grace.

In every action, at all times
Let me enjoy the supreme bliss
Of intoxication from the immortal wine
Resulting from your worship, O Lord.

To the devotees
The meaning of the supreme endeavor of your
    worship
Is quite obvious.
They experience from it
A joy beyond all expectation.

In my opinion,
Not even a trace of the wealth of joy
Is attained until one experiences
The great festival of your worship.

Immersed in worship, the devotees find themselves
Deep within your being
Without effort, without concern
For any accessories.

Nothing remains for them to achieve,
Nothing is difficult for them to obtain:
The devotees wander the earth without purpose,
Drunk only with the joy of worshiping you.

Whose consciousness is expanded
With intense devotion
Has a unique, praiseworthy style of worship
Unsullied by entreaties, O Granter of Boons.

What beauty, what delight,
What other wealth,
Or what other liberation
Does not exist
Where is worshiped the Transcendent Lord?

Nourished by the nectar
Of pure devotion rippling within,
Let my body become fit for your worship.

O Mighty One! Lord of the Worlds!
Although my actions are uniquely unfettered,
I would become unfettered
If indeed it were required
To enjoy your worship.

Those few who while meditating
Thirst for your vision and your touch
Receive the cool, sweet,
Deep lake of your worship.

Just as you
Are the only object of delightful worship
In this world, O Lord,
So also is the devotee
A deserving object of delightful worship.

O Master! How glorious
Is your great festival of worship,
Which reduces to ashes
Even the thirty-six *tattva*s.

Praised be those, O Lord,
Whose water of immortal devotion
Makes worthy of worship
Even the materials of your ceremony.

Having begun to meditate on you with a *mantra*,
Certain of your devotees, O Lord,
Even in their transcendental beings
Cannot contain their ecstacy.

Rejoicing as if they had been made kings,
Certain of your devotees in the festival of worship
Pour out the wine of immortality
Everywhere throughout the world.

Those chosen few whose pleasures entail
The endless imbibing of the nectar of your worship—
Are they gods, or liberated beings,
Or are they something else, O Lord?

Absorbing the universe into themselves
As the materials of worship,
How immeasurably heavy—and yet how light—
Become the devotees!

For devotees, the agitation
Caused by the projection of the senses
When performing worship
Is indeed the source of immortality
Just as the agitation of the ocean of milk
Was for the gods.

Some consider worship as the wish-granting cow
That gratifies all desires,
But others, turning inward,
Drink a milk sweeter than streams of nectar.

Even the projection of senses
Known as this world
Fosters the initiation of the devotees
Into the supreme unearthly festival of worship.

In the heat of intense devotion, O Lord,
Worshiping you as my true self
Does not cause me to be plaintive;
It is, rather, the highest fruit of plaintiveness.

Some consider worship only as a means
Of striving for your state.
But for devotees
It is a process—
During which one enjoys
The sweet bliss of union with you.

Although unconventional, the worship
Of those who have become free
Through delirious devotion—
What a sublime end it reaches!

O Śambhu, you alone
Are the true, wondrous object of worship
That emanates from hearts stunned
By tasting the sweet nectar of devotion.

Master, while engaging in your worship
Let my senses become full, pure, devoted,
And strong.

Immersed in your worship, O Lord,
The absolute treasure of all worship,
Oh, what unearthly splendor
Radiates from the senses.

Such humility
Is truly seen only in you,
O Master, who, even though lord of the universe,
Are worshiped by servants
And are obtained.

Whether out of the concrete or the abstract,
Out of existence or nonexistence,
May the great festival of your worship
Ever radiate in me,
Who have been made worthy of praise.

Adoration to those who, having offered up
All of their desires, anger, and pride,
Perform your worship incessantly.
With them are you truly pleased!

Most glorious
Is this path of worship through devotion,
Which, though performed with pieces of straw,
Is accomplished indeed with jewels.

STOTRA EIGHTEEN

Becoming Clear

O Lord of the Universe!
Only your devotees, having discovered you
From within the universe
Again find the universe as within you,
For nothing in the world is beyond their reach.

You dominate one state;
Another is dominated by Bhavānī,
Pregnant with all of material creation.
Ultimately, there is no difference
Between Devī, the three worlds, and you.

People given to vanity
Do not understand the essence of beauty,
Or indeed that the essence of everything
That exists is beautiful.

Alas, the mind, although eager, even then
Does not realize the essence of the self.
Alas, I am lost!

I bow to him who, having made his dwelling
In his own self, consisting of your essence,
Abounds with the wealth of the worship of your feet
Heedless of food, heedless of cover.

This world, though dwelling comfortably
Within your body,
Is burning within.
Through your own will
Grant that here and now
I may be filled with the bliss of worshiping you.

With mind taken with drinking the nectar
Of worshiping spontaneously
The pair of your lotus feet,
Let me become a pilgrim of the world
Encountering in the accumulation of things
Only bliss.

With you, O Lord, shining clearly
In all worldly transactions,

Let all things appear to me
As constantly coming and going.

Let me forever wander about
Only within you,
Or as one with you.
Let there not be a moment
When I am not glorified as being one with you.

Rich with your worship,
Your devotees frolic
In this ocean of the world
Brimming with the cool nectar
That flows from your limbs.

In the vast forest of your worship,
O Lord, may I, your devotee,
Forever rest in the cool shade
Beneath the tree of Supreme Sound.

O Lord! Appear before me
Adorned with your three eyes
And trident
Just as to all beings
You appear in all things
As light.

I have dedicated my ego to you
As an offering of devotion.
When will you be pleased enough
To become everywhere
The object of my sight?

Dwelling in the ocean of supreme bliss,
With mind absorbed only in your worship,
Let me engage in worldly affairs,
Relishing the ineffable at the same time.

All that is here in this world is yours.
Who could even begin to explain its essence?
Even so, your name, form, and movements
Captivate my heart,
O Captivator as you are!

Those who are filled with devotion
Have not the slightest craving
For happiness as a means to attaining peace.
In the presence of the Heart-captivator,
They do not even remember to pray
For liberation.

Wakefulness, dreaming, or deep sleep—
Whatever the state—

When those who are worthy of devotion
Turn their attention toward you,
All this becomes a great festival.

The modifications of the senses,
Including the mind,
Have such an inconstant nature!
How does one
Who is radiant with the wealth of devotion
Make them become steady, firm, and wise, O Lord?

Nothing that you created is distinct from you,
And nothing that you created is other than bliss.
Yet all is sorrow and disharmony.
May you be glorified,
O Abode of unique bewilderment!

The impurity of differentiation
Having been washed away by the brimming nectar
Filling the abyss of obscuration,
And having trampled doubt, the invincible enemy,
Let me have your vision endlessly.

O Lord, inspire my whole being
So that I may be attached to you always,
And having come extremely close,

Let me worship you intently
In your true form.

No one at all is competent to praise you.
Who could ever begin to speak of your beauty?
But my prayer is always this—
That I may ever behold the Lord.

STOTRA NINETEEN

The Meaning Revealed

Beyond the range of prayer
Is the bestower of wondrous fruit,
The One of unparalleled behavior,
The wishing tree of heaven—
May Śiva be glorified!

Everything in the world is obtained from you,
The single source of the multitude of objects.
Still, to me you do not reveal
Your being as my own self—
It remains afar.

The reality behind everything
Is the conscious being
Who consists of the powers of knowledge and
    action,
The Great Lord.

Otherwise, not even a name would be possible,
Let alone anything else.

O Lord, set me on the path
That destroys dreadful suffering
And leads toward your recognition.
Let me as a result
Attain the state of merging with you.

When shall spiritual perfection
Bejewelled with the memory of your spotless feet
Come from you to me,
Causing awe in the hearts of perfected beings?

O Lord, when shall I behold
Your flawless countenance
Emitting floods of nectar
Drowning the whole world?

When, O Lord, shall your form,
Which appears only in a moment of recollection,
Fill with sublime nectar
The deep abysses that keep me from you?

Intent on the experience of your sublime nectar,
My mind still is not free of unsteadiness.
When will this happen, O Lord?
Oh, may it be soon!

Let me experience
All pairs of opposites
Not as dry and lacking the nectar
Of the bliss of your union,
But as dedicated to you.

O Lord! Let your spotless rays
Shine before me, face to face,
So that the darkness of physical and mental torments
Be completely dispelled.

O Celestial One, grant that I may overcome
The enemies along your path,
The sense-thieves
Who conceal the highest reality.

Soon, O Mighty One, fill my mind
With floods of the nectar of your devotion
So that these vain desires be completely submerged
And swept away.

Why is it, O Unborn One,
That your devotion does not shine
In the state of liberation
To one still bearing mortal characteristics?
Therefore raise me to a state of perfection
Befitting me as I am.

Let me not become proud, O Lord,
In the attainment of mere *siddhis*.
For the radiance of *aṇimā* and the other powers,
And even of liberation itself,
Is but scant in the face of your devotion.

Just this much I pray:
That the Lord be pleased with me, his servant,
Who could never begin to understand
All that has been given
By the Lord of the Three Worlds.

In the lake of my mind, spilling over
With the bliss of the memory of your form,
May the lotuses of the pair of your feet
Ever bloom, effusing
Nectar most delicious and sublime.

This, the Lord, Tryambaka,
Is my father
And Bhavānī is my mother.
To me there is no second in the world.
With this realization
May I wander in the highest ecstacy.

STOTRA TWENTY

The Meaning Savored

I bow to the Master, Lord of the Three Worlds,
White with ashes, three-eyed,
Bearing the serpent as sacred thread
And crescent moon as diadem.

Homage to the one wearing as raiment
His own lustrous halo of radiant beams,
Bedecked with a glittering garland of skulls
For the festival of dance at the end of the world.

I bow to the eternally sacred abodes,
Whose deity is Hara,
Whose activities are worthy of Hara,
And whose very breath of life is dedicated
Only to Hara.

Beyond your lordship is yet another
One of your amusements—
That is, by sheer will I find
Spontaneous means to your glorious acts.

When the whole universe
Honors just this much of your splendor—
The mere play in the world—
How infinite indeed
Must be your bliss!

How can one not be beatified
Who is loved by Gaurī's Hara?
And how can Hara not be
The supreme beloved of Gaurī?

Just as the roots of that sacred tree
Lie in sublime and everlasting recognition,
So too are formed its branches of sense perception.

When the itch for devotion flares up
Worship comes into being
As a great pillar of smearing-stone.

Glory to the Master,
Whose recreation is the act of creation,
Who delights in preservation,

And who rests contentedly,
Satisfied with the meal of the three worlds.

I bow to them, who,
Going nowhere and renouncing nothing,
Yet view all this as your glorious abode.

What else remains to be desired
By those rolling in the wealth of devotion?
For those deprived of it,
What else is worthy of desire?

Where even agonies transform into pleasure
And poison into nectar,
Where the world itself becomes liberation,
That is the path of Śaṅkara.

In the beginning, the middle, or the final stages,
There is no pain for your devotees, O Lord.
Still, we are suffering.
What is this? Tell me!

O Lord, some seek your realization
Through knowledge, through *yoga*,
Or through other disciplines.
But this realization shines forth constantly
Only to the self-willed devotees.

There is no plaintiveness for devotees
Nor any worry,
For their own self is identical with you.
Even then, in the external state
The indescribable word *O Śiva* is on their lips.

O Lord, I praise your Kriyā Śakti,
Light of all lights,
Filled with universal consciousness as
"I am all this."

O Celestial One, all beings,
Including Brahmā, Indra, and Viṣṇu,
View their objects as food.
Therefore, I glorify the universe
As consisting only of you.

Because being and nonbeing are relative,
Everything apart from me is unreal.
This alone is the significance
Of your play of dissolution, O Lord.

By mere recognition, O Granter of Boons,
Does your transcendental form emerge
Before those rolling in the wealth of devotion.
And thus do they conquer all causes of pain.

As though saturated with the wine
Of the nectar of devotion,
With vital organs radiating with delight,
The adventurous ones dance through the night
With Śiva's attendants, a party of ghosts.

With the same devotional mood
In which I began these hymns,
May I, O Śambhu, grow ever more secure.

oṃ